Practice Test for the

Cognitive Abilities Test (CogAT®*) Form 7
Level 14 - (Grade 7-8)
Practice Test 2

A study guide to test into your school's best programs.

Mercer Publishing
PO Box 1075 Mercer Island, WA 98040

* CogAT® is a registered trademark of the Houghton Mifflin Company which was not involved in the production of, and does not endorse, this practice test.

This Book Belongs to

_____

TABLE OF CONTENTS

Table of Contents

What is the Cognitive Abilities Test (CogAT®*) Form 7 Exam?

One of the principal tools for measuring a student's ability to enter their school's gifted program is the Cognitive Abilities Test (CogAT®*) published by Riverside Publishing. The CogAT®* exam is an ability or aptitude test which measures students on their problem solving and reasoning skills. Many of the questions on the CogAT®* exam are types your child would not have seen or done before. Most kids are at a disadvantage if they have not prepared in advance for this exam.

Riverside Publishing's CogAT®* exam is marketed as Canadian Cognitive Abilities Test (CCAT) in Canada (distributed by Nelson Education) and as the CAT in the UK (distributed by GL Assessment).

The CogAT®* exam measures learned problem solving and reasoning skills in three cognitive areas: Verbal, Quantitative and Nonverbal. Although these cognitive areas are included in an IQ test, an IQ test analyses a broader number of areas. While the CogAT®* exam measures some of the same areas, it is not an IQ test. With the focus on problem solving and reasoning, the CogAT®* exam is intended to be a predictor of potential success in school.

Unlike the exams your child is used to taking, questions on the CogAT®* exam may have more than one answer that appears to be correct. Students must use their problem solving and reasoning skills to determine the best answer, not one that could be correct. As an example, if the question was "Which one is an instrument?" and your child is given two choices: a bucket and a trumpet, the correct answer is trumpet. While a bucket could be an instrument in some circumstances (if it is made into a drum), the better answer is trumpet.

Some school districts use students' scores on the CogAT®* exam as the sole eligibility requirement for inclusion, or non-inclusion, into their school's gifted program. Others use the CogAT®* exam in combination with an achievement test, such as the Iowa Test of Basic Skills (ITBS) or the Stanford Achievement Test. Achievement tests measures knowledge in things they have learned in school (like reading and math). Typically, school districts do not use academic performance and achievement test scores without aptitude test scores for eligibility into their school's gifted program. Therefore, being a good student and getting good grades is usually not enough to get into most school's best programs.

In 2011 Riverside Publishing announced the release of Form 7 of the CogAT®* exam. The CogAT®* Form 7 Multilevel Edition exams have been modified from the previous version by replacing some of the test areas on the CogAT®* Form 6 exam with new test areas. Overall changes to the CogAT®* exam are intended to make the exam fairer to ELL (English Language Learner) students.

The CogAT®* exam is a group administered test given to a full classroom of students at a time.

What is included in this book?

This book includes the following:

- Explanations for each of the test areas and sample questions
- One full-length practice test, with the same number of questions as the CogAT®* Level 14 exam (typically given to students in 7th and 8th grades)
- Practice test answers
- Progress chart to track your child's efforts
- Steps for improving your child's scores

How does the practice test in this book correspond with the exam?

The CogAT®* Multilevel Edition Level 14 exam is usually given to students in 7th and 8th grades, and includes the following number of questions at Level 14:

Verbal

Verbal Analogies	24 questions
Sentence Completion	20 questions
Verbal Classification	20 questions

Quantitative

Number Analogies	18 questions
Number Puzzles	16 questions
Number Series	18 questions

Nonverbal

Figure Matrices	22 questions
Paper Folding	16 questions
Figure Classification	22 questions

The practice test in this book includes questions similar in content and format to the questions your child will see on the exam.

The object of the practice test is to familiarize your child with the types of questions they will face on test day, how the tests are formatted, the symbols used and the number of questions in each test area. However, since this practice test has not been standardized with Riverside Publishing and the actual CogAT®* exam, a valid CogAT®* score cannot be concluded from the results on this practice test.

How should this book be used?

The Practice Test for the Cognitive Abilities Test (CogAT®*) Form 7 - Level 14 book is designed to use for children in 7th and 8th grade preparing for the CogAT®* Form 7 Level 14 exam. The concepts and questions in this book can also be used to prepare children for other types of cognitive or reasoning tests, such as the Otis-Lennon School Ability Test (OLSAT).

We recommend that parents sit with their children when doing the practice test to ensure they understand what the questions are asking rather than letting your child get an entire section wrong and then telling them at the end. This reinforces doing the questions correctly each time they use the practice test so there will not be confusion on the day of the exam.

To answer the questions, we recommend that children use our CogAT®* Form 7 bubble test form (exclusively available on the Mercer Publishing website) to simulate the actual exam, however we have included a location to enter the answer after each question if your child is not using the bubble test form. These answer locations in our practice test workbooks are not included on the actual exam.

There are nine test areas on the CogAT®* Form 7 exam. How you approach studying for the exam depends on how much time you have before the exam - many parents are given little (if any) warning that their child will be tested and others have months to prepare.

We recommend completing the first practice test by starting at the beginning and completing the test areas in order. Depending on the amount of time you have, this could be done over the course of an evening or spread across days or weeks.

Read through the directions for each subtest and do the sample questions with your child to ensure they understand how the questions in that subtest are formatted and what the question is asking. Then begin the practice test. If your child does not answer the first questions correctly, stop the practice test and go back to the directions and sample questions. Then repeat the first questions in the practice test to ensure they understand the questions in that section.

Answers are included at the back of the practice test. Determine the number of correct answers your child had in each test area and review the progress chart at the back of this book to determine your child's percentage of correct answers.

Review the Steps for Improving Scores section for tips and suggestions on how to improve your child's scores on the practice test.

If you have purchased a second practice test, save the second practice test to have your child do right before the exam. We find that many of the smart children who are taking these exams memorize the answers to the questions in the practice test they have completed and, therefore, need a different practice test so their child will think through the questions rather than reciting the memorized answer.

What materials do we need to do the practice test?

To perform the practice test in this book, your child will need the following:

- **A parent or administrator (recommended).** Multilevel Ed. exams expect that children can read and answer the questions themselves. We recommend that parents sit with their children when doing the practice test to ensure they understand what the questions are asking.
- **The practice test included in this book.**
- **A pencil and eraser.**
- **Mercer Publishing's CogAT®* Form 7 bubble test form (recommended).** Exams are often scored electronically using bubble test forms. Many children have never seen a bubble test form prior to exam day and errors can be made from using the form incorrectly. Children can mark the correct answer in the wrong bubble and circles that are incorrectly filled in or answer sheets that contain stray marks may negatively impact your child's score on the exam. While it is not required, we highly recommended your child use our bubble test form when they do our practice test to simulate the exam. Our CogAT Form 7 bubble test forms are exclusively available on the Mercer Publishing website.

What else can we do to improve my child's score?

Once your child takes our practice test, there are several proactive steps that you can take that may increase your child's score. We have included a progress chart and a Steps for Improving Scores section devoted to this topic.

Mercer Publishing has a full set of materials in The Gifted Program® Series to help your child score as well as they can on their gifted program entrance exam.

For more on available materials, visit our website at www.mercerpublishing.com.

Now, on to the practice test.

* CogAT® is a registered trademark of the Houghton Mifflin Company which was not involved in the production of, and does not endorse, this practice test.

Practice Test 2

Verbal Analogies

Directions

In the Verbal Analogies subtest, students are given a pair of words and another word without its pair. The first pair of words is related in some way. Students must determine how they are related and then select the word from the available answers that has the same relationship with the third word.

Sample Questions

1.

big → biggest : small →

A. tiny   B. smallest   C. elfin   D. weak   E. young

In this analogy, the first pair is big and biggest – biggest is form of big used when comparing three or more items. In the second pair, you are given small and must select the word that has the same relationship as the first pair. The form of small you would use when comparing three or more items is…

The correct answer is B. smallest. B is the answer you would mark on the bubble test form or in the available answer field*.

2.

finger → hand : toe →

A. foot   B. polish   C. toenail   D. leg   E. ankle

In this analogy, the first pair is finger and hand – a finger is part of a hand. In the second pair, you are given toe and must select the word that has the same relationship as the first pair. Toe is part of a…

The correct answer is A. foot. A is the answer you would mark on the bubble test form or in the available answer field*.

* Answer fields will not be in your child's exam workbook. Bubble test forms are typically used during the exam and marking your answers on a bubble test form as they do the practice test is recommended.

Begin

1. light → dark : rough →

   A. gloomy   B. difficult   C. lucky   D. minor   E. smooth

   Answer: _____

2. January → November : October →

   A. July   B. August   C. December   D. Halloween   E. March

   Answer: _____

3. inch → yard : pint →

   A. ounce   B. mile   C. liquid   D. centimeter   E. gallon

   Answer: _____

4. sink → down : lift →

   A. drain   B. pool   C. station   D. up   E. in

   Answer: _____

Continue

5. crying → sad : yelling →

    A. despair   B. angry   C. shouting   D. fleeing   E. revenge

                Answer: _____

6. steal → stole : eat →

    A. consume   B. dinner   C. ate   D. missing   E. calories

                Answer: _____

7. cowboy → boot : athlete →

    A. sport   B. trophy   C. sneaker   D. helmet   E. team

                Answer: _____

8. creek → river : hill →

    A. mountain   B. mound   C. sea   D. canoe   E. valley

                Answer: _____

Continue →

9. cook → knife : soldier →

    A. battle   B. rifle   C. hero   D. victory   E. enemy

                                        Answer: _____

10. Mexican → burrito : Italian →

    A. donkey   B. pasta   C. wine   D. Rome   E. countryside

                                        Answer: _____

11. sun → star : Earth →

    A. planet   B. moon   C. Saturn   D. galaxy   E. telescope

                                        Answer: _____

12. hand → finger : piano →

    A. tune   B. song   C. palm   D. music   E. keys

                                        Answer: _____

Continue

13. simple → complex : addition →

    A. subtraction   B. calculation C. exam   D. algebra   E. complicated

Answer: _____

14. wallet → money : pool →

    A. cue   B. table   C. water   D. swimming E. swimsuit

Answer: _____

15. true → fiction : history →

    A. class   B. teacher   C. book   D. myth   E. fact

Answer: _____

16. soup → cake : appetizer →

    A. shrimp   B. dinner   C. dessert   D. ice cream E. snack

Answer: _____

Continue ⇨

17. dog → wolf : cat →

    A. Siamese   B. poodle   C. feline   D. prey   E. jaguar

    Answer: _____

18. apples → orchard : grapes →

    A. wine   B. vineyard   C. green   D. bottle   E. raisins

    Answer: _____

19. thick → rope : thin →

    A. spidery   B. tie   C. cable   D. string   E. wispy

    Answer: _____

20. soup → spoon : celery →

    A. knife   B. fingers   C. vegetables   D. stalk   E. chunks

    Answer: _____

Continue ▷

21. napkin → mouth : towel →

A. dry   B. body   C. lips   D. shower   E. dinner

Answer: _____

22. nap → sleep : snack →

A. time   B. hamburger   C. eat   D. awake   E. bed

Answer: _____

23. house → paint : skin →

A. lotion   B. sunburn   C. protection   D. fur   E. shirt

Answer: _____

24. strategy → plan : success →

A. defeat   B. final   C. ultimate   D. triumph   E. money

Answer: _____

STOP!

Sentence Completion

Directions

In the Sentence Completion subtest, students are given a sentence that is missing a word. Students must determine which of the available answers best completes the sentence.

Sample Questions

1.

The dog _____ at the delivery man.

   A. mooed   B. meowed   C. yelled   D. frowned   E. barked

The correct answer is E. barked. E is the answer you would mark on the bubble test form or in the available answer field*.

2.

Ice cream _____ if it doesn't stay cold.

   A. tires   B. melts   C. licks   D. freezes   E. enjoys

The correct answer is B. melts. B is the answer you would mark on the bubble test form or in the available answer field*.

* Answer fields will not be in your child's exam workbook. Bubble test forms are typically used during the exam and marking your answers on a bubble test form as they do the practice test is recommended.

1. The bully was sent to the principal's office because of his _____ behavior.

    A. deviant   B. helpful   C. tardy   D. stylish   E. unfortunate

    Answer: _____

2. The boys were too _____ , so their mother told them to be quite.

    A. shy   B. noisy   C. negative   D. weird   E. hungry

    Answer: _____

3. Jeff was _____ when he won the $5,000 grand prize in the contest.

    A. calm   B. dissatisfied   C. splurging   D. surprised   E. distracted

    Answer: _____

4. When the two rival groups met up on that hot Saturday night in August, they created quite a _____.

    A. fight   B. party   C. heat wave   D. construction   E. thunderstorm

    Answer: _____

Continue

5. Boats and planes are used to _____ many goods.

    A. heat   B. transport   C. sell   D. remove   E. order

                                      Answer: _____

6. Unfortunately, our bathrooms will not _____ people in wheelchairs.

    A. remove   B. seat   C. like   D. accommodate   E. turn

                                      Answer: _____

7. Greg preferred the _____ colors of flowers to the drab earth tones of trees.

    A. monotone   B. floral   C. dark   D. vibrant   E. loud

                                      Answer: _____

8. The aroma of dinner cooking made the hikers _____ .

    A. tired   B. sore   C. hungry   D. scramble   E. angry

                                      Answer: _____

Continue

9. When the king's brother was murdered, the king wanted _____ .

   A. dinner   B. revenge   C. money   D. festivities   E. fury

   Answer: _____

10. The thieves found themselves in a difficult _____ when the homeowners came home early.

    A. cell   B. remove   C. predicament   D. presentation   E. trick

    Answer: _____

11. Many toxic chemicals are _____ to your health.

    A. useful   B. hazardous   C. internal   D. prescribed   E. recommended

    Answer: _____

12. She used a safety pin as a _____ button.

    A. makeshift   B. perfect   C. computer   D. purchased   E. fastened

    Answer: _____

Continue

13. The doctor urged the patient not to worry because the results were only
_____ .

A. ordered   B. positive   C. harmful   D. preliminary   E. concise

Answer: _____

14. Stephen needed to _____ a new strategy because he had no idea what to do next.

A. formulate   B. discard   C. restart   D. buy   E. find

Answer: _____

15. The military commanders decided to _____ additional troops in order to stop the enemy advance.

A. interview   B. banish   C. deploy   D. create   E. thank

Answer: _____

16. Gregory planned to go to the beach but decided to change his _____ and go to the carnival with friends instead.

A. clothes   B. plans   C. memory   D. schedule   E. links

Answer: _____

Continue

17. Our water supply is running out, so we need to _____ as much as possible.

    A. use   B. conserve   C. drink   D. find   E. waste

                              Answer: _____

18. To evolve, you must _____ to change.

    A. hide   B. design   C. strategize   D. adapt   E. hunt

                              Answer: _____

19. The bride's _____ was made from the finest imported materials.

    A. father   B. cake   C. presents   D. gown   E. church

                              Answer: _____

20. She felt a great sense of _____ when she got to the top of the mountain and saw the natural beauty around her.

    A. awe   B. wind   C. riches   D. resentment   E. attractiveness

                              Answer: _____

Verbal Classification

Directions

In the Verbal Classification subtest, each question has two rows of words. In the top row, the student is given a set of three words that are similar in some way. Students must determine how they are similar and then select the word from the available answers that is most similar to the words on the top row.

Sample Questions

1. yellow   purple   green

    A. caterpillar   B. brown   C. chalk   D. pretty   E. colorful

The correct answer is B. brown. B is the answer you would mark on the bubble test form or in the available answer field*.

2. triangle   diamond   oval

    A. ball   B. circle   C. shape   D. baseball   E. character

The correct answer is B. circle. B is the answer you would mark on the bubble test form or in the available answer field*.

*   Answer fields will not be in your child's exam workbook. Bubble test forms are typically used during the exam and marking your answers on a bubble test form as they do the practice test is recommended.

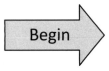

1. alone   isolated   separated

   A. problematic   B. merry   C. difficult   D. miserable   E. apart

   Answer: _____

2. den   attic   closet

   A. roof   B. tower   C. hall   D. chandelier   E. mezzanine

   Answer: _____

3. brain   ear   sinus

   A. leg   B. wig   C. cheek   D. cap   E. house

   Answer: _____

4. hardwood   tile   carpet

   A. glass   B. linoleum   C. cabinets   D. furnace   E. vent

   Answer: _____

Continue

5. desktop   icon   memory

    A. pencil   B. file   C. school   D. student   E. desk

                                            Answer: _____

6. soccer   football   hockey

    A. score   B. stadium   C. baseball   D. player   E. referee

                                            Answer: _____

7. volume   size   length

    A. capacity   B. ruler   C. shape   D. box   E. square

                                            Answer: _____

8. wrench   hammer   pliers

    A. wood   B. nail   C. metal   D. house   E. screwdriver

                                            Answer: _____

Continue ⟹

9. positive   sure   guaranteed

A. negative   B. certain   C. help   D. doubt   E. free

Answer: _____

10. roof   peak   penthouse

A. ceiling   B. appendix   C. conclusion   D. hole   E. start

Answer: _____

11. statute   rule   regulation

A. judge   B. ticket   C. law   D. courthouse   E. convict

Answer: _____

12. den   map   out

A. score   B. game   C. spy   D. hoax   E. gone

Answer: _____

Continue

13. country   rock   blues

A. city   B. pasture   C. guitar   D. jazz   E. radio

Answer: _____

14. distress   suffering   misery

A. rage   B. restless   C. amusement D. drowsy   E. anguish

Answer: _____

15. adjective   preposition   noun

A. grammar   B. sentence   C. apostrophe   D. period   E. verb

Answer: _____

16. week   decade   second

A. calendar   B. clock   C. century   D. pendulum E. end

Answer: _____

Continue

17. boxer   ninja   gladiator

    A. helper   B. wrestler   C. ring   D. winner   E. retriever

                                   Answer: _____

18. asthma   arthritis   allergies

    A. anger   B. hospital   C. autism   D. injury   E. patient

                                   Answer: _____

19. chart   map   plans

    A. trip   B. book   C. diagram   D. photo   E. appendix

                                   Answer: _____

20. window   porthole   telescope

    A. pitcher   B. monitor   C. microwave   D. skylight   E. door

                                   Answer: _____

Number Analogies

Directions

In the Number Analogies subtest, students are given two pairs of numbers and another number without its pair. The first two pairs of numbers are related in some way. Students must determine how they are related and then select the number from the available answers that has the same relationship with the number in the third pair.

Sample Questions

1. [2 → 2] [4 → 4] [6 → ?]

    A. 3   B. 4   C. 5   D. 6   E. 7

The correct answer is D. 6. D is the answer you would mark on the bubble test form or in the available answer field*.

2. [2 → 1] [5 → 4] [8 → ?]

    A. 4   B. 5   C. 6   D. 7   E. 8

The correct answer is D. 7. D is the answer you would mark on the bubble test form or in the available answer field*.

---

* Answer fields will not be in your child's exam workbook. Bubble test forms are typically used during the exam and marking your answers on a bubble test form as they do the practice test is recommended.

Begin

1. [9 → 3]   [23 → 17]   [11 → ?]

    A. 2   B. 3   C. 4   D. 5   E. 6

                                                Answer: _____

2. [4 → 14]   [8 → 26]   [0 → ?]

    A. 0   B. 2   C. 4   D. 6   E. 8

                                                Answer: _____

3. [18 → 8]   [22 → 10]   [32 → ?]

    A. 12   B. 13   C. 14   D. 15   E. 16

                                                Answer: _____

4. [6 → 12]   [28 → 78]   [11 → ?]

    A. 7   B. 12   C. 17   D. 22   E. 27

                                                Answer: _____

Continue

5. [5 → 7]   [2 → 1]   [8 → ?]

    A. 12   B. 13   C. 14   D. 15   E. 16

Answer: _____

6. [24 → 3]   [15 → 0]   [36 → ?]

    A. 5   B. 7   C. 8   D. 11   E. 12

Answer: _____

7. [9 → 6]   [18 → 12]   [3 → ?]

    A. 0   B. 2   C. 4   D. 6   E. 8

Answer: _____

8. [16 → 5]   [4 → 1]   [25 → ?]

    A. 4   B. 7   C. 8   D. 11   E. 12

Answer: _____

Continue →

9. [10 → 60]   [13 → 78]   [7 → ?]

   A. 34   B. 36   C. 38   D. 40   E. 42

Answer: _____

10. [6 → 22]   [5 → 20]   [8 → ?]

   A. 25   B. 26   C. 27   D. 28   E. 29

Answer: _____

11. [11 → 23]   [6 → 18]   [7 → ?]

   A. 13   B. 15   C. 17   D. 19   E. 21

Answer: _____

12. [10 → 6]   [4 → 3]   [12 → ?]

   A. 7   B. 9   C. 11   D. 13   E. 15

Answer: _____

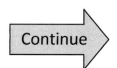

Continue

13. [45 → 11]   [33 → 7]   [21 → ?]

    A. 3   B. 4   C. 5   D. 6   E. 7

Answer: _____

14. [11 → 132]   [8 → 96]   [4 → ?]

    A. 40   B. 42   C. 44   D. 46   E. 48

Answer: _____

15. [10 → 20]   [12 → 26]   [4 → ?]

    A. 2   B. 4   C. 6   D. 8   E. 10

Answer: _____

16. [18 → 5]   [10 → 1]   [24 → ?]

    A. 4   B. 6   C. 8   D. 10   E. 12

Answer: _____

Continue →

17. [12 → 8]   [6 → 2]   [11 → ?]

   A. 5   B. 7   C. 9   D. 11   E. 13

                                                   Answer: _____

18. [0 → 1]   [3 → 10]   [7 → ?]

   A. 16   B. 18   C. 20   D. 22   E. 25

                                                   Answer: _____

Number Puzzles

Directions

In the Number Puzzles subtest, students are given a mathematical equation and students must determine the number from the available answers that should replace the question mark in the equation.

Sample Questions

There are two types of questions that may be found in the number puzzles subtest:

1. (2 + 2) + 2 = (2 + ?) + 2

    A. 2   B. 4   C. 6   D. 8   E. 10

The correct answer is A. 2. A is the answer you would mark on the bubble test form or in the available answer field*.

2. 4 + ■ = ?

    ■ = 2

    A. 2   B. 4   C. 6   D. 8   E. 10

In this number puzzles problem, the student must substitute the value for ■ (2) in the equation to determine the value for the question mark. The correct answer is C. 6. C is the answer you would mark on the bubble test form or in the available answer field*.

* Answer fields will not be in your child's exam workbook. Bubble test forms are typically used during the exam and marking your answers on a bubble test form as they do the practice test is recommended.

 Begin

1. ? x 2 = ■ + 4

   ■ = 2 x 4

   A. 2   B. 4   C. 6   D. 12   E. 20

   Answer: _____

2. 35 ÷ ? = ▲

   ▲ x 4 = 20

   A. 3   B. 5   C. 6   D. 7   E. 9

   Answer: _____

3. ◆ + 9 = ?

   ◆ + 14 = 18

   A. 6   B. 8   C. 10   D. 13   E. 14

   Answer: _____

4. ● + 6 = ◆ ÷ ?

   ● - 4 = 6
   ◆ = 8 x 4

   A. 2   B. 3   C. 4   D. 5   E. 6

   Answer: _____

Continue

5. ● + 3 = ○ - ?

    ● - 6 = 2
    ○ ÷ 2 = 7

    A. 0   B. 1   C. 2   D. 3   E. 4

Answer: _____

6. ● ÷ 2 = ◇ - ?

    ● + 3 = 7
    ◇ ÷ 2 = 3

    A. 3   B. 4   C. 5   D. 6   E. 7

Answer: _____

7. 17 - ◇ = ● + ?

    ◇ + 6 = 9
    ● x 3 = 15

    A. 6   B. 7   C. 8   D. 9   E. 10

Answer: _____

8. 4 x ◆ = ? - ○

    ◆ = 21 ÷ 7
    ○ = 2 + 1

    A. 11   B. 12   C. 13   D. 14   E. 15

Answer: _____

Continue ⟹

9. ◆ ÷ ? = ● - ☐

   ◆ = 2 x 10
   ● = 4 + 2
   ☐ = 4 ÷ 2

   A. 2   B. 3   C. 4   D. 5   E. 6

   Answer: _____

10. ? + ● = ◇ - ○

    ◇ = 9 x 3
    ○ = 2 x 5
    ● = 2 + 2

    A. 13   B. 14   C. 15   D. 16   E. 17

    Answer: _____

11. ? - ■ = ○ x ◆

    ■ = ◆ ÷ 2
    ○ = ■ + 1
    ◆ = 4

    A. 14   B. 15   C. 16   D. 17   E. 18

    Answer: _____

12. ◆ - ○ = ? + ■

    ◆ = 10 + 13
    ○ = 4 x 3
    ■ = (○ ÷ 2) + 4

    A. 1   B. 3   C. 6   D. 9   E. 12

    Answer: _____

Continue

13. ○ - ? = □ + 3
    ○ = 4 x □
    □ = 3

A. 4   B. 6   C. 8   D. 10   E. 12

Answer: _____

14. ? = ▲ - 3
    ● + ● = ▲
    ▲ x ● = 32

A. 3   B. 4   C. 5   D. 6   E. 8

Answer: _____

15. ▲ - ? = ◇ - ▲
    ? + ◇ = 7 x 2
    ◇ = ▲ + 2

A. 1   B. 2   C. 3   D. 4   E. 5

Answer: _____

16. ● + ? = □ x ●
    ? + □ = 13 x 2
    □ = ● + 2

A. 14   B. 16   C. 18   D. 20   E. 24

Answer: _____

STOP!

Number Series

Directions

In the Number Series subtest, the student is shown a series of numbers. Students need to review the numbers to determine the rule or pattern used and then select the number from the answer choices that should come next in the series.

Sample Questions

1. 1   2   3   4   5 →

    A. 4　　　　B. 5　　　　C. 6　　　　D. 7　　　　E. 8

The correct answer is C. 6. C is the answer you would mark on the bubble test form or in the available answer field*.

2. 0   5   0   5   0 →

    A. 5　　　　B. 7　　　　C. 0　　　　D. 3　　　　E. 6

The correct answer is A. 5. A is the answer you would mark on the bubble test form or in the available answer field*.

*   Answer fields will not be in your child's exam workbook. Bubble test forms are typically used during the exam and marking your answers on a bubble test form as they do the practice test is recommended.

1. 28 25 22 19 16 →

    A. 10   B. 11   C. 12   D. 13   E. 14

    Answer: _____

2. 9 11 15 17 21 23 27 →

    A. 33   B. 25   C. 27   D. 31   E. 29

    Answer: _____

3. 62 65 61 64 60 63 →

    A. 59   B. 60   C. 61   D. 62   E. 64

    Answer: _____

4. 9 13 8 12 →

    A. 7   B. 8   C. 9   D. 10   E. 11

    Answer: _____

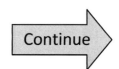

5. 1/2 2/5 3/8 4/11 →

   A. 1/4   B. 5/14   C. 1/2   D. 1/3   E. 5/15

   Answer: _____

6. 27 28 30 33 38 45 56 →

   A. 66   B. 67   C. 68   D. 69   E. 70

   Answer: _____

7. 5 6 8 11 15 →

   A. 9   B. 13   C. 20   D. 22   E. 24

   Answer: _____

8. 5 7 11 17 →

   A. 19   B. 21   C. 23   D. 25   E. 27

   Answer: _____

Continue

9.   4   12   18   22   →

A. 22   B. 24   C. 26   D. 28   E. 30

Answer: _____

10.   27   26   28   25   29   24   30   →

A. 20   B. 23   C. 25   D. 29   E. 34

Answer: _____

11.   5   8   10   11   13   16   →

A. 16   B. 18   C. 20   D. 21   E. 23

Answer: _____

12.   36   99   18   33   9   →

A. 11   B. 16   C. 24   D. 36   E. 72

Answer: _____

Continue

13. 4 1 3 9 6 8 →
-3 +2 +6 -3 +2 +6

    A. 7   B. 11   C. 14   D. 16   E. 19

Answer: _____

14. 1 1 3 9 5 →

    A. 1   B. 9   C. 11   D. 17   E. 25

Answer: _____

15. 11 8 8 13 10 10 →
-3 0 5 -3 0 -5

    A. 11   B. 12   C. 13   D. 14   E. 15

Answer: _____

16. 0 0 0 1 4 16 2 →
×4 ×4 ×4

    A. 0   B. 3   C. 8   D. 24   E. 36

Answer: _____

Continue

17. 654 754 764 765 865 875 →

     A. 857   B. 876   C. 885   D. 957   E. 975

                                                    Answer: _____

18.   432 431 421 321 320 →

     A. 220   B. 302   C. 310   D. 311   E. 319

                                                    Answer: _____

Figure Matrices

Directions

In the Figure Matrices subtest, each question is a matrix or grid divided into sections. Each section contains a either a shape, figure or question mark. Students must determine which of the available answers would best replace the question mark to complete the matrix. Questions usually come it two types: Figure Analogy or Pattern Completion.

Sample Questions

1. Figure Analogy

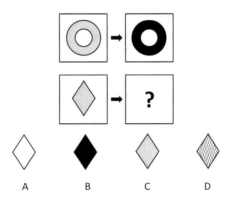

The correct answer is B. B is the answer you would mark on the bubble test form or in the available answer field*.

2. Pattern Completion

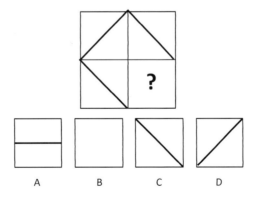

The correct answer is D. D is the answer you would mark on the bubble test form or in the available answer field*.

* Answer fields will not be in your child's exam workbook. Bubble test forms are typically used during the exam and marking your answers on a bubble test form as they do the practice test is recommended.

Begin

1.

A   B   C   D   E

Answer: _____

2.

A   B   C   D   E

Answer: _____

Continue

3.

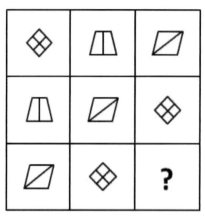

A   B   C   D   E

Answer: _____

4.

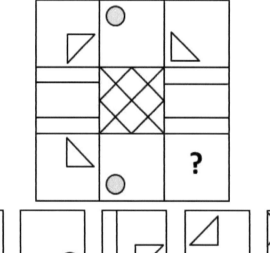

A   B   C   D   E

Answer: _____

5.

A   B   C   D   E

Answer: _____

6.

A   B   C   D   E

Answer: _____

Continue

7.

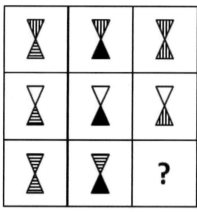

A   B   C   D   E

Answer: _____

8.

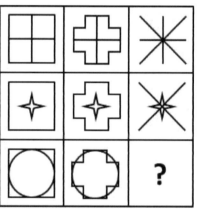

A   B   C   D   E

Answer: _____

9.

A   B   C   D   E

Answer: _____

10.

A   B   C   D   E

Answer: _____

Continue

11.

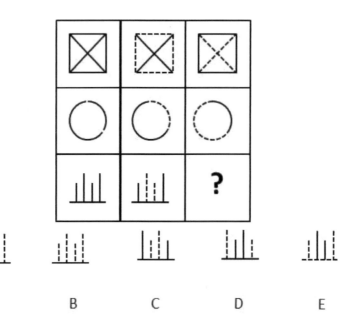

A   B   C   D   E

Answer: _____

12.

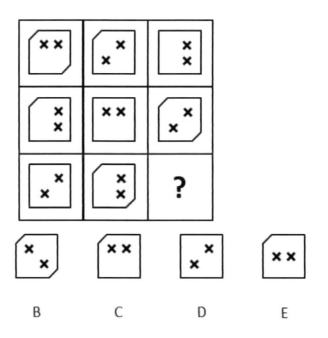

A   B   C   D   E

Answer: _____

Continue

13.

A   B   C   D   E

Answer: _____

14.

A   B   C   D   E

Answer: _____

Continue

15.

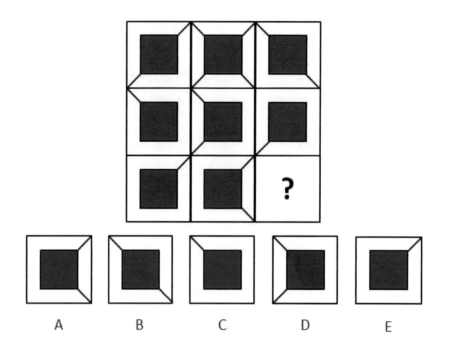

A   B   C   D   E

Answer: _____

16.

Answer: _____

Continue

17.

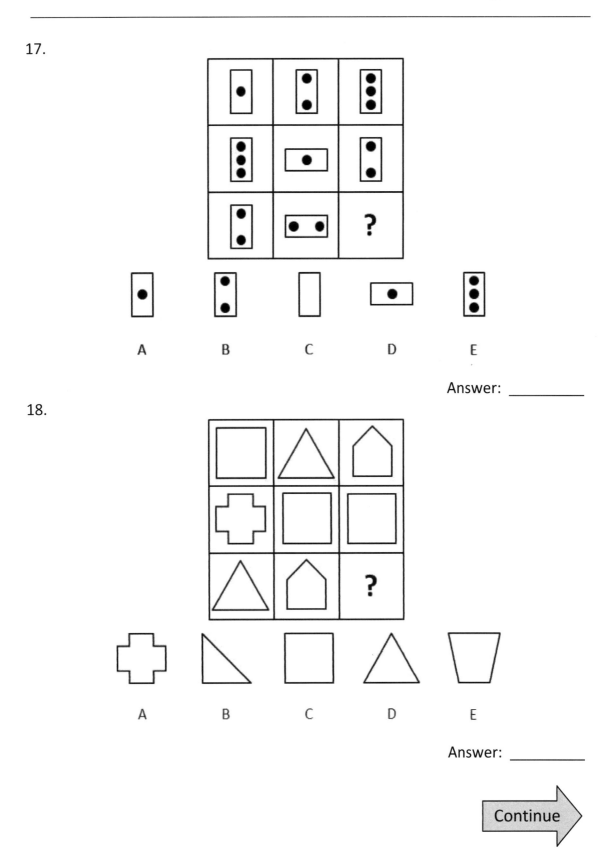

A   B   C   D   E

Answer: _____

18.

A   B   C   D   E

Answer: _____

Continue

19.

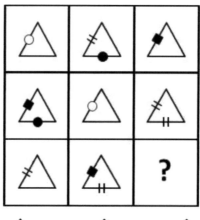

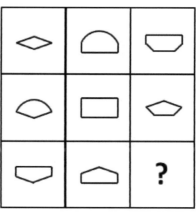

A   B   C   D   E

Answer: _____

20.

A   B   C   D   E

Answer: _____

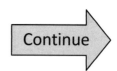
Continue

21.

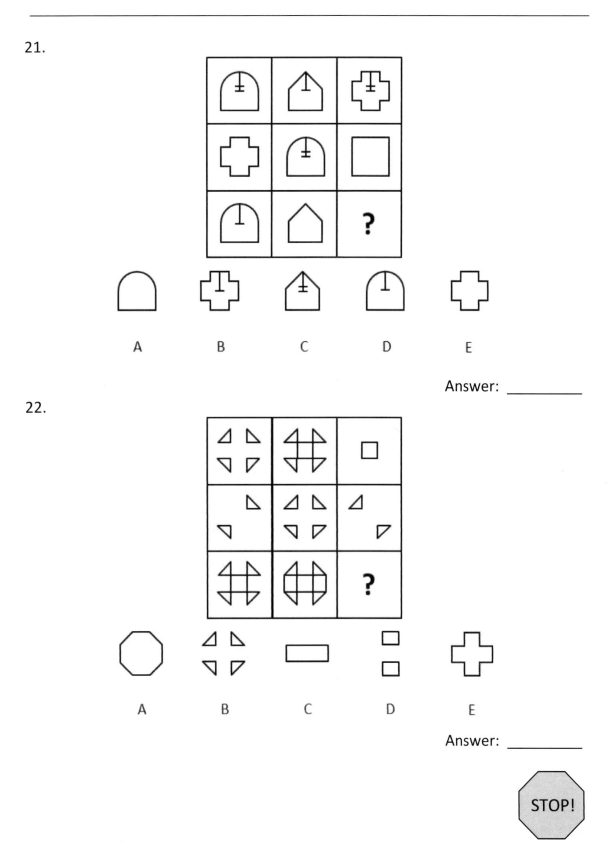

Answer: _____

22.

Answer: _____

STOP!

Paper Folding

Directions

In the Paper Folding subtest, each question shows a square piece of paper being folded and then the folded paper is hole-punched. Select the answer from the bottom row that shows how the folded paper with holes will look when it is unfolded.

Sample Question

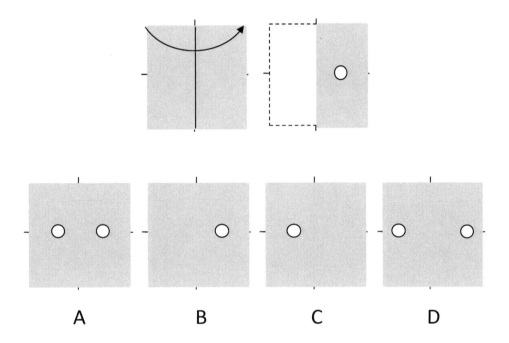

A   B   C   D

The correct answer is A. A is the answer you would mark on the bubble test form or in the available answer field*.

---

* Answer fields will not be in your child's exam workbook. Bubble test forms are typically used during the exam and marking your answers on a bubble test form as they do the practice test is recommended.

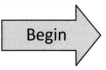

1.

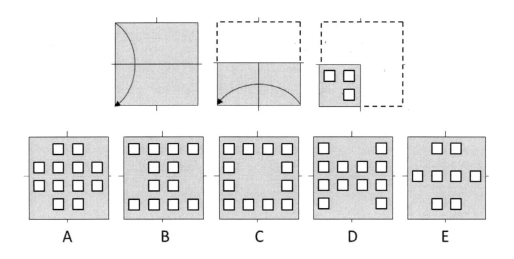

Answer: _____

2.

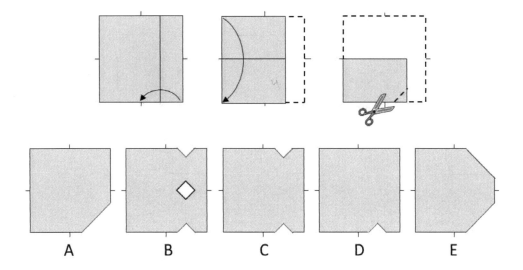

Answer: _____

Continue

3.

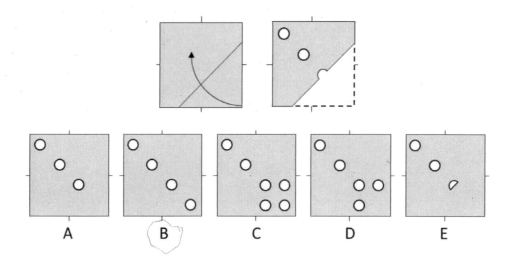

Answer: _____

4.

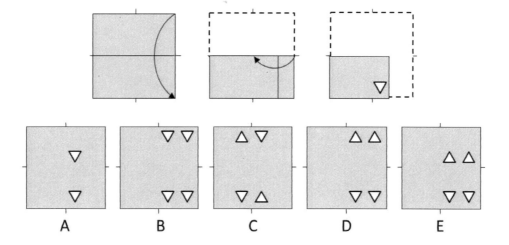

Answer: _____

Continue

5.

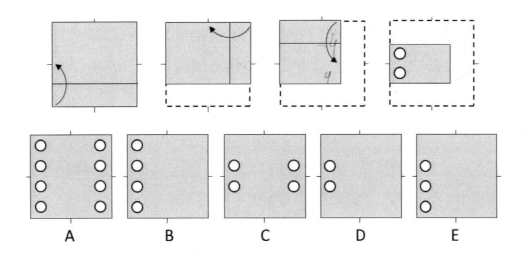

Answer: _____

6.

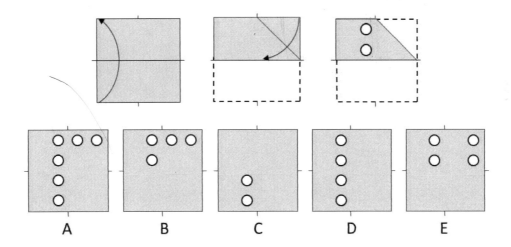

Answer: _____

Continue

7.

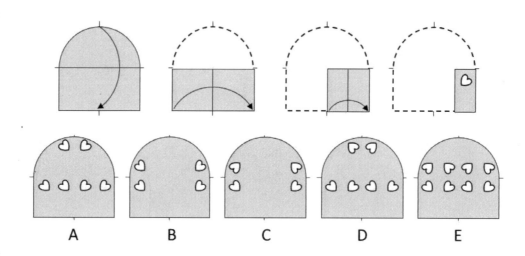

Answer: _____

8.

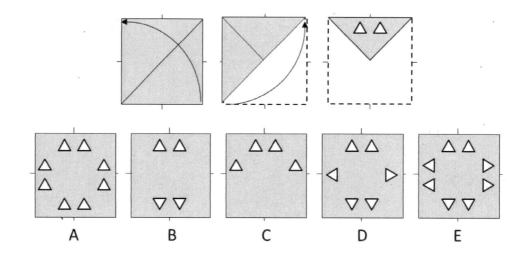

Answer: _____

Continue

9.

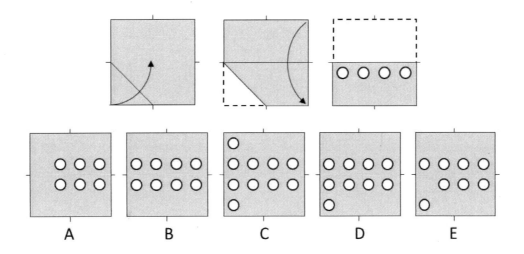

Answer: _____

10.

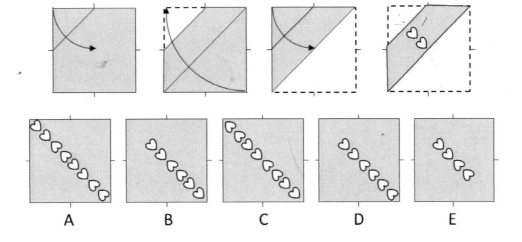

Answer: _____

Continue

11.

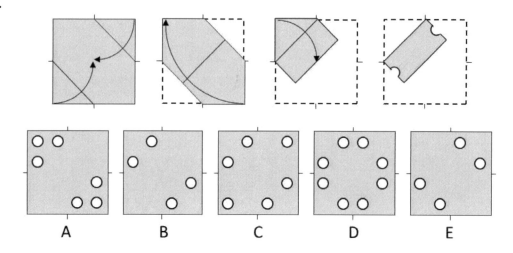

Answer: _____

12.

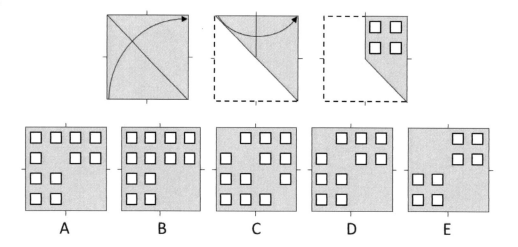

Answer: _____

Continue

13.

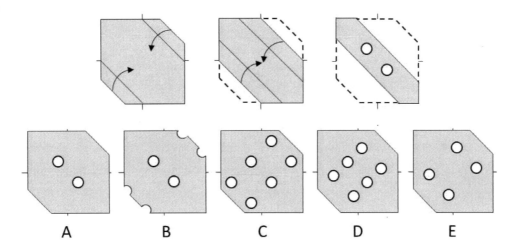

Answer: _____

14.

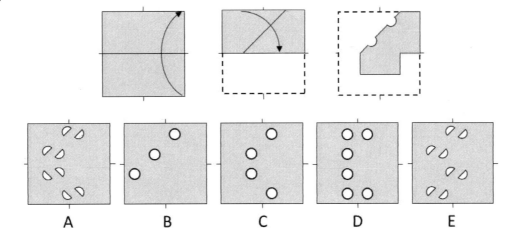

Answer: _____

15.

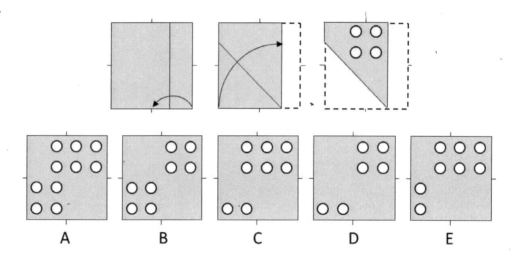

A   B   C   D   E

Answer: _____

16.

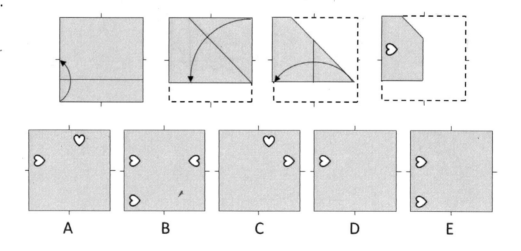

A   B   C   D   E

Answer: _____

STOP!

Figure Classification

Directions

In the Figure Classification subtest, each question has two rows of figures. In the top row, the student is given a set of three figures that are similar in some way. Students must determine how they are similar and then select the figure from the available answers that is most similar to the pictures on the top row.

Sample Question

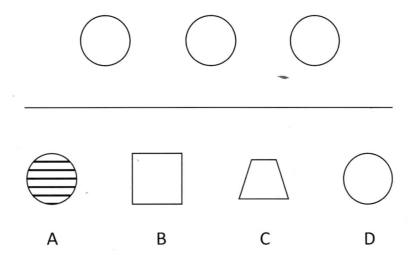

The correct answer is D, the white circle. D is the answer you would mark on the bubble test form or in the available answer field*.

---

*   Answer fields will not be in your child's exam workbook. Bubble test forms are typically used during the exam and marking your answers on a bubble test form as they do the practice test is recommended.

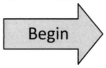

1.

A   B   C   D   E

Answer: _____

2.

A   B   C   D   E

Answer: _____

Continue →

3.

_____

A   B   C   D   E

Answer: _____

4.

_____

A   B   C   D   E

Answer: _____

Continue

5.

Answer: _____

6.

Answer: _____

7.

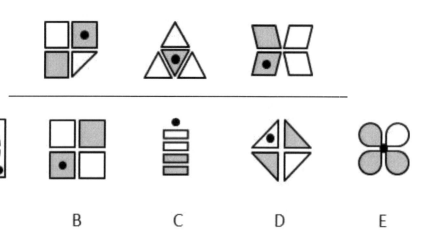

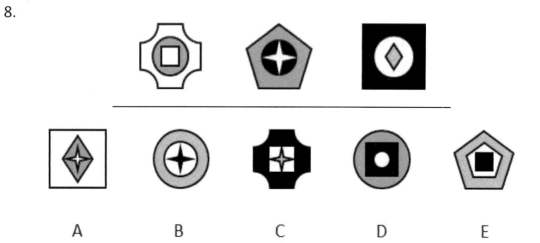

A   B   C   D   E

Answer: _____

8.

A   B   C   D   E

Answer: _____

Continue

9.

Answer: _____

10.

Answer: _____

Continue

11.

Answer: _____

12.

Answer: _____

Continue

13.

A   B   C   D   E

Answer: _____

14.

A   B   C   D   E

Answer: _____

Continue

15.

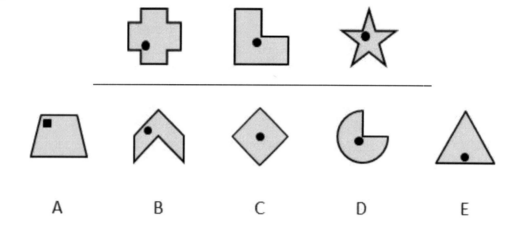

A   B   C   D   E

Answer: _____

16.

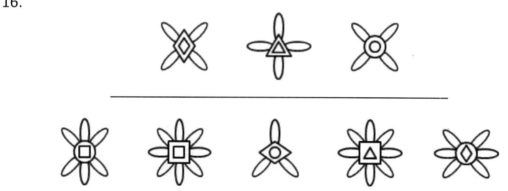

Answer: _____

Continue

17.

A   B   C   D   E

Answer: _____

18.

A   B   C   D   E

Answer: _____

Continue

19.

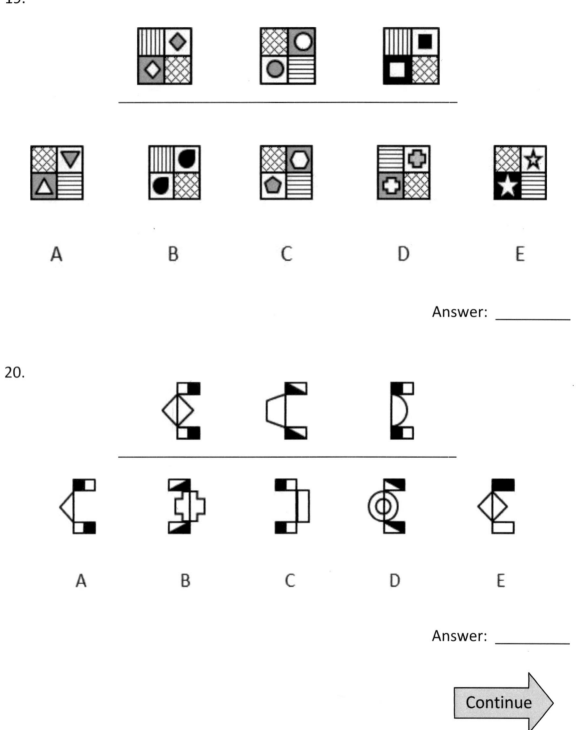

A   B   C   D   E

Answer: _____

20.

A   B   C   D   E

Answer: _____

Continue

21.

A   B   C   D   E

Answer: _____

22.

A   B   C   D   E

Answer: _____

Verbal Analogies

1.	E	smooth	Both pairs of words are opposites of each other.
2.	B	August	January is 2 months after November and October is 2 months after August.
3.	E	gallon	Inches are a smaller measure of length than a yard and pints are a smaller measure of liquid than gallons.
4.	D	up	Sink is a movement down and lift is a movement up.
5.	B	angry	Crying is a common response to being sad and yelling is a common response to being angry.
6.	C	ate	Steal is the present tense of stole and eat is the present tense of ate.
7.	C	sneaker	Both are about footwear – a cowboy wears a boot and an athlete wears a sneaker.
8.	A	mountain	A creek is a very small river and a hill is a very small mountain.
9.	B	rifle	A cook uses a knife and a soldier uses a rifle.
10.	B	pasta	A burrito is a food from Mexico and pasta is a food from Italy.
11.	A	planet	The sun is a star and Earth is a planet.
12.	E	keys	Fingers are a component of a hand and keys are a component of a piano.
13.	D	algebra	Addition is relatively simple form of math and algebra is more complex form of math.
14.	C	water	Money is put in a wallet and water is put in a pool.
15.	D	myth	History is true account of the past and a myth is fictional account of the past.
16.	C	dessert	Soup is generally eaten at the beginning of a meal and cake is generally eaten at the end. The general word for something eaten at the beginning is appetizer and the general word for something eaten at the end is dessert.
17.	E	jaguar	A wolf is a wild animal in the same family as a dog and a jaguar is a wild animal in the same family as a cat.
18.	B	vineyard	Apples are grown in an orchard and grapes are grown in a vineyard.
19.	D	string	Rope is thicker than similarly constructed string.

20.	B	fingers	Soup is eaten with a spoon and celery is eaten with your fingers.
21.	B	body	A napkin is generally used to wipe one's mouth and a towel is generally used to wipe one's body.
22.	C	eat	Sleep is the action performed during a nap and eat is the action performed during a snack.
23.	A	lotion	Paint is applied to a house and lotion is applied to skin.
24.	D	triumph	To plan is to have a strategy and to triumph is to have success.

Sentence Completion

1.	A	deviant
2.	B	noisy
3.	D	surprised
4.	A	fight
5.	B	transport
6.	D	accommodate
7.	D	vibrant
8.	C	hungry
9.	B	revenge
10.	C	predicament
11.	B	hazardous
12.	A	makeshift
13.	D	preliminary
14.	A	formulate
15.	C	deploy
16.	B	plans
17.	B	conserve
18.	D	adapt
19.	D	gown
20.	A	awe

Verbal Classification

1.	E	apart	Classification:	Synonyms.
2.	C	hall	Classification:	Names of areas within a house.
3.	C	cheek	Classification:	Parts of a head.
4.	B	linoleum	Classification:	Types of flooring.
5.	B	file	Classification:	Words associated with computers.
6.	C	baseball	Classification:	Team sports.
7.	A	capacity	Classification:	Forms of measurement.
8.	E	screwdriver	Classification:	Tools.
9.	B	certain	Classification:	Synonyms.
10.	A	ceiling	Classification:	Things that are on top.
11.	C	law	Classification:	Synonyms.
12.	C	spy	Classification:	All words are spelled with 3 letters.
13.	D	jazz	Classification:	Types of music.
14.	E	anguish	Classification:	Synonyms.
15.	E	verb	Classification:	Parts of speech.
16.	C	century	Classification:	Specific intervals of time.
17.	B	wrestler	Classification:	Names of fighters.
18.	C	autism	Classification:	Illness/Disease that start with the letter "A".
19.	C	diagram	Classification:	Synonyms.
20.	D	skylight	Classification:	Things a person can see through.

Number Analogies

1.	D	5	Subtract 6 from the first number to get the second number.
2.	B	2	Multiply the first number by 3 and add 2 to get the second number.
3.	D	15	Divide the first number by 2 and subtract 1 to get the second number.
4.	E	27	Multiply the first number by 3 then subtract 6 to get the second number.
5.	B	13	Multiply the first number by 2 and subtract 3 to get the second number.
6.	B	7	Divide the first number by 3 and subtract 5 to get the second number.
7.	B	2	Multiply the first number by 2/3 to get the second number.
8.	C	8	Subtract 1 from the first number and divide by 3 to get the second number.
9.	E	42	Multiply the first number by 6 to get the second number.
10.	B	26	Add 5 to the first number and multiply by 2 to get the second number.
11.	D	19	Add 12 to the first number to get the second number.
12.	A	7	Divide the first number by 2 and add 1 to get the second number.
13.	A	3	Subtract 12 from the first number and divide by 3 to get the second number.
14.	E	48	Multiply the first number by 12 to get the second number.
15.	A	2	Multiply the first number by 3 and subtract 10 to get the second number.
16.	C	8	Divide the first number by 2 and subtract 4 to get the second number.
17.	B	7	Subtract 4 from the first number to get the second number.
18.	D	22	Multiply the first number by 3 and add 1 to get the second number.

Number Puzzles

1.	C	6
2.	D	7
3.	D	13
4.	A	2
5.	D	3
6.	B	4
7.	D	9
8.	E	15
9.	C	4
10.	A	13
11.	A	14
12.	A	1
13.	B	6
14.	C	5
15.	E	5
16.	D	20

Number Series

1.	D	13	Subtract 3 from each number to get the next number.
2.	E	29	Add 2 to the first number to get the second number, add 4 to the second number to get the third. Repeat starting with the third number.
3.	A	59	Add 3 to the first number to get the second number, subtract 4 from the second number to get the third. Repeat starting with the third number.
4.	A	7	Add 4 to the first number to get the second number, subtract 5 from the second number to get the third. Repeat starting with the third number.
5.	B	5/14	Pattern in a fraction - Increase the numerator by 1 and increase the denominator by 3 of each number to get the next number.
6.	D	69	Increasing addition - 1, 2, 3, 5, 7, 11, 13 (prime numbers). Add 1 to the first number to get the second. Add 2 to the second number to get the third. Increase the number to add to the next prime number each time.
7.	C	20	Increasing addition - 1, 2, 3, 4. Add 1 to the first number to get the second. Add 2 to the second number to get the third. Increase the number to add by 1 each time.
8.	D	25	Increasing addition - 2, 4, 6, 8. Add 2 to the first number to get the second. Add 4 to the second number to get the third. Increase the number to add by 2 each time.
9.	B	24	Decreasing addition – 8, 6, 4, 2. Add 8 to the first number to get the second. Add 6 to the second number to get the third. Decrease the number to add by 2 each time.
10.	B	23	Pattern in the number added - -1, +2, -3, +4... Add -1 (subtract 1) to the first number to get the second. Add 2 to the second number to get the third. Increase the number to add by one each time and subtract every other time.
11.	B	18	Pattern in the number added - 3, 2, 1, 2, 3... Add 3 to the first number to get the second. Add 2 to the second number to get the third. Follow the pattern of the number added (3, 2, 1, 2, 3).

12.	A	11	Every other number- Divide the first number by 2 to get the third number, divide the second number by 3 to get the forth number. Repeat starting with the fourth number.
13.	C	14	Pattern in the number added - -3, +2, +6, -3, +2, +6... Add -3 to (subtract 3 from) the first number to get the second. Add 2 to the second number to get the third. Add 6 to the third number to get the fourth. Follow the pattern of the number added (-3, +2, +6).
14.	E	25	Sets of 2 - Square the first number in each set (multiply it by itself) to get the second number of each set. Add 2 to the first number in the set to get the first number of the next set (the third number). Repeat starting with the third number.
15.	E	15	Sets of 3 - Subtract 3 from the first number to get the second number. Add 0 to the second number to get the third completing the first set of 3. Add 2 to the first number in the first set to get the first number in the next set. Repeat starting with the fourth number.
16.	C	8	Sets of 3; Multiply the first number in the set by 4 to get the second number. Multiply the second number in the set by 4 to get the third number completing the first set of 3. Add one to the first number in the first set to get the first number in the second set. Repeat starting with the fourth number.
17.	B	876	Pattern within a number - Increase the hundreds digit of the first number by one to get the second number. Increase the tens digit of the second number by one to get the third. Increase the ones digit of the third number by one to get the fourth number. Repeat starting with the fourth number.
18.	C	310	Pattern within a number - Decrease the ones digit of the first number by one to get the second. Decrease the tens digit of the second number by one to get the third. Decrease the hundreds digit of the third number by one to get the fourth. Repeat starting with the fourth number.

Figure Matrices

1. B   Serial Reasoning   The figure ⬍ is placed in the pattern ▦. The figure ⊕ is placed in the pattern ▦ and the figure ⊞ is placed in the pattern ▦.

2. E   Figure Analogy   To get the figure in the second column squares are added to the figure in the first column - two squares are added to squares the third column and one square is added to the squares in the fourth column.

To get the figure in the third column squares are removed from the figure in the second column - one square is removed from the squares in the second column.

3. E   Serial Reasoning   The figure ▱ is placed in the pattern ▦. The figure ▯ is placed in the pattern ▦ and the figure ◊ is placed in the pattern ▦.

4. A   Pattern Completion

5. D   Serial Reasoning   The figure ⊞ is placed in the pattern ▦. The figure ⊟ is placed in the pattern ▦ and the figure ⊟ is placed in the pattern ▦.

6. E   Figure Analogy.   To get the figure in the second column, the two left shapes in the first column figure change position. To get the figure in the third column, the top left shape of the figure in the *first* column has its color changed to gray.

7. C   Serial Reasoning   The upper triangle ▽ is placed in the pattern ▦ . The upper triangle ▽ is placed in the pattern ▦ and the upper triangle ▽ is placed in the pattern ▦.

The lower triangle ▽ is placed in the pattern ▦ . The lower triangle ▲ is placed in the pattern ▦ and the lower triangle is placed in the pattern ▦.

8.	E	Serial Reasoning	The figure + is placed in the pattern ⊞. The figure ✦ is placed in the pattern ⊞ and the figure ○ is placed in the pattern ⊞.

The figure ☐ is placed in the pattern ⊞. The figure ✦ is placed in the pattern ⊞ and the figure ✕ is placed in the pattern ⊞.

9.	E	Pattern Completion	The figures are in pairs going around the outside cells starting with the top left and top middle figures. The pair that includes the missing figure also includes the bottom middle figure.
10.	E.	Serial Reasoning	The figure ⊞ is placed in the pattern ⊞. The figure ⊞ is placed in the pattern ⊞ and the pattern ⊞ is placed in the pattern ⊞.

The figure ⊞ is placed in the pattern ⊞. The pattern ⊞ is left blank and the figure ⊞ is placed in the pattern ⊞.

11.	E.	Figure Analogy	To create the figure in the third column, the solid lines in the second column figure are changed to dashed and the dashed lines are changed to solid.
12.	C	Serial Reasoning	The outer figure ☐ is placed in the pattern ⊞. The outer figure ☐ is placed in the pattern ⊞ and the outer figure ☐ is placed in the pattern ⊞.

The figure ×× is placed in the pattern ⊞. The figure ×ˣ is placed in the pattern ⊞ and the figure ˣ× is placed in the pattern ⊞.

Practice Test 2
Answers

_____

13.   D.   Figure Analogy   The figure ☐ is placed in the pattern ▦. The figure ◠ is placed in the pattern ▦ and the figure ○ is placed in the pattern ▦.

In each column, the quadrants in the first two rows are replicated in the figure in the third row.

14.   E   Figure Analogy   Each figure is a combination of shapes and whether the two shapes are overlapping or not.

In each row, the combination of shapes in the first column is flipped in the third column.

In each column, if the first row has overlapping shapes, the shapes in the second and third rows are not overlapping. If the first row does not have overlapping shapes, the shapes in the second and third rows are overlapping.

15.   A.   Figure Analogy   The figure in the second column is created from the items of the figures in the first and third columns. Items that are in either the first or third column are repeated in the second column.

16.   B   Pattern Completion.   The figure ⌉ is placed in the pattern ▦ and the figure ⌈ is placed in the pattern ▦. The "best" answer would be replicating the figure ⊢ placed in the pattern ▦.

17.   C   Figure Analogy   Numbers in the first and second column are added to get the number in the third column. Rectangles that are vertical are positive and rectangles that are horizontal are negative.

18.   A   Pattern Completion   There are five figures as you go across the rows. Starting with the sixth figure, the five figures are repeated.

19.   E   Serial Reasoning

Each figure is in the shape of a triangle, with one side replaced.
The left side is replaced with ⌐ in the pattern ⊞. . The left side is replaced with ⌐ in the pattern ⊞ and replaced with ⌐ in the pattern ⊞.

The bottom side is left as line in the pattern ⊞. The bottom side is replaced with ⌐ in the pattern of ⊞ and replaced with ⌐ in the pattern ⊞.

20.   C   Serial Reasoning

The figure ⌐ is placed in the top position in the pattern ⊞. The figure ⌒ is placed in the top position in the pattern ⊞ and the figure ⌒ is placed in the top position in the pattern ⊞.

The figure ⌣ is placed in the bottom position in the pattern ⊞. The figure ⌣ is placed in the bottom position in the pattern ⊞ and the figure ⌣ is placed in the bottom position in the pattern ⊞.

21.   B   Pattern Completion

Each figure is a combination of two figures – an outer and inner figure.

In each column, the outer figure in the first row is repeated in the third row.

In each row, the inner figure of the first column is repeated in the third column.

22.   C   Figure Analogy

The figures in the first and third columns are combined to create the figure in the second column.

Practice Test 2
Answers

Paper Folding

1. A
2. C
3. B
4. D
5. B
6. D
7. E
8. E
9. D
10. C
11. E
12. B
13. C
14. C
15. E
16. D

Figure Classification

1. D   All figures in the group have a horizontal and vertical line separating the figure into quarters. One quarter of the figure is shaded and all four quarters are equal in size.

2. E   All figures in the group have the same center shapes – a white diamond with an inner black circle.

3. D   All figures in the group have two of the same shapes – a full outer shape and the inner shape with one side missing.

4. A   All figures in the group are made of the same three shapes – a diamond, square and circle.

5. E   All figures in the group are a rotation of the same figure.

6. C   All figures in the group reverse the colors (white, gray or black) of the shapes (outer and center shapes) in the second cell of the figure.

7. B   All figures in the group are made up of shapes that are either white or shaded. In addition, a black dot is placed in one of the shaded shapes.

8. B   All figures in the group have a circle as the middle shape.

9. C   All figures in the group include a circle, a square, a rectangle and a dot. The dot is in both the rectangle and the square, but not the circle.

10. C   Each figure is made of four shapes lined up vertically. All figures in the group have the two bottom shapes a mirror image of the top two shapes.

11. C   There are two figures. All figures in the group are one of those two figures.

12. D   All figures in the group include a T with a rectangle, circle and two lines in the shape of a V which points toward the perpendicular line in the T. The rectangle, circle and V can be in any order.

13. A   All figures in the group are a rotation of the same figure.

14. B   All figures in the group have lines in the outer and middle shapes that are perpendicular – if the outer shape is horizontal then the middle shape has vertical lines and vice versa.

15. D   All figures in the group have a round circle/dot next to an interior angle that is pointing toward the center of the figure.

16. B   All figures in the group have matching center shapes (both are diamonds, triangles, circles or squares).

17. B   All figures in the group are made up of three different shapes – no two shapes in a figure are the same.

18. D   All figures in the group consist of a grid and three +. The figures in the group do not have a + in the center cell.

19. A   All figures in the group are in a four cell matrix. The top right and bottom left cells have the same shape and the shade of the shape and background are reversed (this excludes answer choices B, C and E). The top left and bottom right are a diamond pattern and a line pattern. If the line pattern is on the top it is vertical; if it is on the bottom, it is horizontal.

20. D   All figures in the group include a rectangle at the top and bottom of the figure that are on the right side of the center line. The rectangles in a single figure are identical (this excludes answer choices A and E).

21. D   All figures in the group have a bottom branch that starts on the left and alternate black and white branches, starting with black on the bottom branches.

22. C   Each figure has two shapes with center objects. All figures in the group have a center shape that is black within the outer shape that has the most sides/corners and a white center shape in the other shape. Both answers A and C fit these criteria. In addition, none of the center shapes match the corresponding outer shapes.

Progress Chart

Follow your progress as you complete the practice test by using the chart below. As you complete each subtest, total the number of correct answers and color in the number in the appropriate column.

When you have completed all of the subtests, use the percentage of correct answers with the information from the Steps to Improve Scores in the next section.

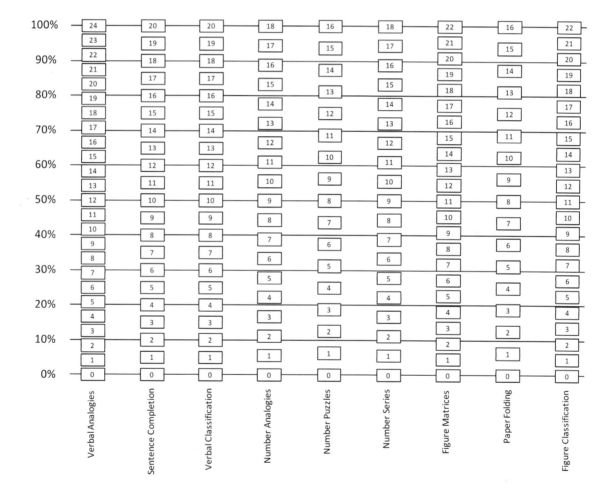

*   This practice test has not been standardized with Riverside Publishing and the actual CogAT® exam. Therefore, a valid CogAT® score cannot be concluded from the results on this practice test.

Steps to Improve Scores

Once your child takes one of our practice exams, there are several proactive steps that you can take that may increase your child's score. Depending on the size of the program at your school and the applicant pool, most schools take the top 1 - 5% of applicants. If your child scores below the 90th percentile on the exam, the chances are very low that your child will be eligible for their school's gifted program.

Each child is different, has different skills and abilities, and each child will react differently to tests, practice tests and instruction. Over the years, we have compiled through our own research and feedback from parents, what works.

Step 1 – Review the Practice Test You Completed

If your child answered any questions wrong, have them try those questions again. If your child guessed on any questions, have them try those questions again as well. Reread all the questions and have your child give a reason why they answered the question the way they did. This level of review and understanding will help your child process the concepts of the test area. Like most things, practice and repetition are extremely helpful.

Step 2 – Don't Panic if Your Child Scores Poorly on the First Practice Test.

Most kids have never taken a test like this. The questions and concepts may be foreign to how your child thinks and processes information. You may notice that after the first several questions in a section, your child's success rate starts to improve. Be patient with your child and let them learn what is being asked; their scores will improve with practice. Many parents have reported to us that their child's scores improved by as much as 50% after using our materials.

Step 3 - Additional Practice Questions

If your child received 80% or higher score on our exam, consider pushing them to take a practice test at the next grade level. The other Multilevel Ed. exams have the same types of questions as the questions in this practice test, but the questions become more difficult as they increase in level.

If your child scored under 80% after a couple of attempts at the test, you might consider purchasing Mercer Publishing's How To Guides (See our website at www.mercerpublishing.com). These guides have effective step-by-step instructions as well as additional practice activities for core skills tested on the CogAT®* exam. These guides are designed to increase your child's skills and confidence.

Step 4 – Be Ready, Physically, on Exam Day.

This sound obvious but it surprises us how many times a child is not physically prepared to take the exam. A smart child who is tired or hungry may not score as well as they could on the exam.

- Get a good night's sleep before the exam – preferably 9 or 10 hours. Less sleep means the child will need to use energy reserves to get through the day.
- Eat a healthy breakfast which includes fruit and complex carbohydrates – like whole grain bread or cereal. This balance creates a more constant stream of energy your child will need to stay focused. High sugar cereals, donuts, and sugar drinks will cause your child's blood sugar to fall dramatically during the exam eroding their focus.
- Make sure your child uses the restroom before the exam. Many schools will not allow your child to go to the restroom during the exam. Children who have to go to the restroom and are not allowed to go are distracted from the exam and may not do as well as they could.
- Parents need to be calm and supportive. As a parent, you have done all you can by using these practice tests and tools. You have ensured that your child understands what each subtest is asking and practiced questions with them. Most children understand that this is an important exam, but added pressure from parents will increase their test anxiety.

MERCER

PUBLISHING

Mercer Publishing understands how important it is to ensure your children are given the opportunities they deserve when it comes to their education. One of the greatest opportunities your child will have is entering their school's gifted program, if they can qualify for the program based on their gifted program entrance test scores.

We provide practice test books for gifted program entry exams that offer:

- Similar questions and test formats to the actual tests
- Full length practice tests
- Answer keys

These books and practice materials are invaluable tools for your child to do their best - and get into their school's best programs!

Please visit our website to find out the current practice test materials that are available.

www.mercerpublishing.com